*T*his book is a gift ̶ had been on my boc ̶ death! Carol Collin ̶ brings guidance and ̶ and recovery that each of us must travel. If your heart is aching with grief today, Carol's words will soothe (some of) the pain and turn you toward the comfort that God alone can give.

~ *Dr. Bryan Eckleman, Pastor, St. Andrews Church*

*C*arol Collins has had more than her share of deep personal loss. Having done the grief work and made it to the other side, she shares her moving and insightful journey. A must read for anyone in the trenches of grief. ~ *Elaine Ehret, MFT*

I have walked closely with a family member through the depth of pain that comes with death. Grieving is a long, hard journey. I know this book will bring comfort to the hurting.

~ *Helen Smallbone, Author, podcaster and mother of Grammy winning artists, "For King and Country" and Rebecca Saint James*

*M*ost everyone has experienced the loss of a loved one. The journey through it is lonely and, at times, desperate. Carol's book is written from the heart of someone who has walked through the pain and redemption of great loss. This book is a treasure for those seeking faith in times of great loss.

~ *Michael Smith, Artist Manager*

*T*his a wonderful book of healing. The reader feels the raw edge of loss softened by the kindly presence of a dear friend beside them, and the covering of God's mercy surrounding them. *A Season of Grief* makes comfort and courage come alive, and I believe any and all will be blessed by Carol's story and the practice of these wisdoms.

~ *Dr. Monte Pries, Author & Licensed Clinical Psychologist*

Carol DeMars Collins

A
Season
of
Grief

Surviving the
Loss of a Loved One

Layout and design by Susan Neas.

All Scripture quotations in this book were
taken from the Holy Bible, NIV version.

A limited printing. Printed in the USA.

Author's E-mail: cdcollinspublishing@gmail.com

$17.99
ISBN 978-0-578-33105-8
51799>

9 780578 331058

For my children
David, Stacia and Steven

He heals the brokenhearted
and binds up their wounds
Psalm 147:3

FOREWORD

At the start of my surgical practice, a loving patient of mine gave me Carol DeMars Collins' book, *Good Morning, God.* This would serve to be the greatest and most meaningful gift of my career. From that moment, it became my daily devotion each morning before I started my surgeries. While caring for my patients who put their trust in me, I also trusted God to guide me. Every day of my work life the thoughtful words I read from Carol became the fuel for the start of my morning. She has and continues to remarkably impact me on a daily basis.

One evening, I emailed her hoping to obtain more of her books. I had given my copy to a patient whose world was shattered when she lost her mother. By the grace of God, Carol answered my email and unbeknownst to me, she lived in the same city. She welcomed me into her home and we both shared our stories of grief. I often refer to Carol as my "prayer angel on earth sent personally from Jesus." Since then, Carol published *Love Notes to God* which became the hope I needed during the pandemic.

Carol has now blessed us with her greatest work to date, *A Season of Grief.* In this book, she shares her own experience with loss, and guides us through a heartfelt journey towards "purpose and light." Whether loss has been endured personally, or if someone you care about has lost a loved one, *A Season of Grief* will create a positive change during the most inconceivable time. The effect of Carol's perspective reveals the incalculable love and grace from God that is indelibly present, epic and massive.

Bao-Thy N. Grant, DDS
Board-certified Oral & Maxillofacial Surgeon

Hope is the thing that perches in the soul
and sings the tunes without words
and never stops at all.

~

Emily Dickinson

INTRODUCTION

Grief is not just a moment in time. It is a journey and every journey is unique. However, our hearts are all seeking the same destination. The unfolding richness of hope, healing and abundant joy.

In this book, you will discover excerpts from the journals I kept while grieving for my loved one. I have also included things I learned along the way. My prayer is they will resonate with you and be of help as you navigate this difficult road.

I could not have traveled my journey without the comfort and compassion of my loving Lord. He was faithful, sitting beside me as I cried, constantly urging me to keep on keeping on. Eventually, in His timing, He led me into a different life, one filled with purpose and light. I am grateful.

Wandering lonely through the sky,
I gently push the clouds apart.
Searching, wondering where you are,
I miss you, my love.

~

CD

DARK DAYS

In the early days of my grief, I would sit in a chair by the window. I could look out and see the trees and grass. It was October. The grass had turned brown and many of the trees had lost their leaves. This seemed to be a metaphor for what I was feeling. I would wrap myself in my husband's robe as I sat there. I could feel his warmth and smell his sweet scent. For what seemed to be hours, my faithful golden retriever, Gypsy, and I would mourn for my husband and Gypsy's master.

As I sat in the chair each morning, I began to experience God in a way I never had. He became my Comforter, Confidant and Friend. He spoke to me in so many ways - especially through His Word. I would look for verses and read them over and over, asking God to help me apply them. I found verses for depression, anxiety, loneliness, fear, frustration, pain and worry. I was on a collision course for all these emotions.

I began to look forward to my daily visits with God. He became my dearest Friend, my Father with whom I could cry and share my innermost thoughts. The Lord was my hope and support during my dark days. He is there for you as well, dear friend. His hand is reaching for yours this very moment.

Where you used to be,
there is a hole in the world,
which I find myself constantly
walking around in the daytime
and falling in at night.
I miss you.

~

Edna St. Vincent Millay

SHOCK

It's happened. After months of suffering, my husband has lost his battle to the insidious disease called cancer. I now realize I have a gaping hole in my heart, but I will have to deal with that later. For now, I am having an out-of-body experience called shock. The Lord is wrapping His arms around me and I am feeling strong and safe. I go through the motions of making phone calls to family, friends and the mortuary. I comfort everyone as they are trying to comfort me.

On the day of the service, I am smiling and calm. It's been over a week since my husband died, and I have yet to shed a tear. I'm still in shock. However, I know this out-of-body experience will not last. I'm about to be on a roller coaster of feelings and emotions called grief.

Can you relate, dear friend? Your experience may be very different from mine. Shock is a welcome gift in the early moments, days, or perhaps even a few weeks. As the numbness and shock begins to wear off, the pain will arrive; deep pain that never seems to subside.

The helpless feelings you have are normal. You are not losing your mind. You are beginning to confront the gaping hole in your heart. It will take time and effort to work through your emotions and the heartache of grief. Please be patient with yourself and ask God to help you. He is just waiting for you to call his name.

*Tears are the water that will dampen
the soil from which you will blossom.*

~

Unknown

PROCESSION OF TEARS

Today I am feeling a very lonesome lull. Everyone around me is returning to their normal lives, while I have just joined the procession of tears. My world has been torn apart and I feel that I, too, have died a death.

The tears I held in for so long have broken through the dam. I cannot control the sobbing and it frightens me. I never imagined I could cry this hard. Will the sobbing ever cease? I finally stop struggling and give in to the pain. The tears subside for a moment, and then the next wave arrives.

I learned, dear friend, that I could not control these bursts of grief. I also learned they were helping me. After I cried, for what seemed to be hours, I would feel refreshed and somewhat peaceful. Tears are a psychological salve. When we put salve on a wound, it aids the healing process. So, let your tears flow. Crying is not a sign of weakness, rather it is the power to propel you forward. Why do you hurt so? It's because you have loved so.

Our gracious Lord is sitting beside you as you cry. He wants to gather you in His arms as He would a little lamb. He longs to comfort you. He loves you, my friend. You are His most prized possession.

We must dare to pray even as we doubt.
True faith is like a light that begins to flicker,
however faintly in the darkness that beckons us
to pray even when we can hardly
find the words to pray.

~

Jerry Sittser

DENIAL

My mind is playing tricks on me. There are times when I think I must be dreaming. Tonight, I am certain I heard the garage door open, signaling the return of my husband from his office. Then I remembered, he is no longer physically with me. I must be in denial. Denial, grief's strongman, is helping me pretend this dreadful thing did not happen.

There is grace in denial, especially in the early days of grief. Denial helps you pace your feelings. I could not handle very much because it was hard to comprehend what had happened. To fully believe this dreadful thing would be much too overwhelming. Give yourself grace, my friend. Eventually, denial will fade away and you will face the hard fact of your loved one's passing.

Denial is a way of managing the anxiety you may be feeling. Because your life has been altered drastically, you will probably grasp the changes very slowly. In time, as you begin to wrestle with the reality of what has happened, you will cautiously begin to move forward. It might be one step forward and two steps back for a while, but slowly the process of acceptance will begin.

The loss of a loved one is life's most stressful event. However, with support and patience, you will survive. In the meantime, please take care of yourself. Proper nutrition, sleep, and a balance of quiet time and activity will aid in your healing.

Even in the darkest moments of my grief, I found clear signs of God's presence. Lean on Him, dear friend. His promises never fail.

When we are no longer
able to change a situation,
we are challenged to change ourselves.

~

Viktor Frankel

BARGAINING

I feel desperate, like I am losing control. In my desperation, I wonder if I could have done things differently. I am crying out to God and pleading with Him to bring my husband back. Could I just have a few more minutes alone with my husband to tell him how much he meant to me? Why did I leave these things unsaid? Lord, if you will fix this, I promise to be a better person.

Bargaining is a natural response to grief. Our minds constantly grapple with reality. Despair and anxiety seemed to roll into one as I played the blame game.

There were many days when I would dwell on what I might have done to prevent my loved one's death. I desperately wanted to change things. "What if" scenarios crowded my mind day after day after day.

I felt like I was fighting an uphill battle and I did not want to surrender. Over and over, as I continued to fight, I told myself I could change the outcome. However, I came to the conclusion the odds were against me. It was time to wave the white flag of resignation.

God was my reason to surrender, and He is yours as well. He longs to fight your battles. When your emotions are overwhelming and you see no way out, He is waiting on the sideline to come to your rescue. Trust Him, dear friend.

"Come let's settle the matter," says the Lord.
"Though your sins are scarlet,
they shall be white as snow."

~

Isaiah 1:18

REGRET AND REMORSE

Today I find myself sinking into the quicksand of "what ifs." What if I had urged you to go to the doctor sooner? What if we had gotten a second opinion? Why wasn't I more patient with you? Why didn't I say, "I love you," one more time?

How about you, dear friend? Do you have similar questions?

We are only human, and humans have regrets. This applies to everything in life. Second-guessing ourselves over the events of our loved one's death keeps the guilty feelings in our thoughts and can create a roadblock to healing.

When we lose someone very close to us, it's only natural to feel remorseful over things we wish we could change. Sometimes, we even imagine we could have prevented the death. Let me ask you a question. Do we really have that much power? I came to the conclusion that doing things differently may have changed the process of my husband's death. However, it would *not* have changed the outcome.

If you truly feel there are things you could have said or done differently, why not apologize? You can write your loved one a letter or you can just say it in your heart. Please know, like myself and many others, we did the very best we could. I'm certain our loved one knew that.

God understands our emotions and He knows our hearts. Why not talk your guilty feelings over with Him? You will be glad you did.

*Faith isn't the ability to
believe long and far into the future.
It's simply taking God at His word
and taking the next step.*

~

Joni Eareckson Tada

ANGER

Today, I am asking questions. Why has this dreadful thing happened to me? What about the dreams for my future? Why am I left all alone? Whose fault is this? I am angry and I want answers. My stability has been shattered and I feel robbed. What can I do about it?

These are questions we sometimes ask ourselves and there are no clear-cut answers. Anger is a natural emotion we all feel at times, grieving or not. We are hurting and the fury is bubbling to the surface. Anger is a trap door that turns into blame and may be a cover-up for fear. It's important to not bottle up our emotions. We must let them out so as not to lose our wholeness.

How did I overcome my obsession with anger? I had to get to the point that I was tired of fighting and I wanted to let it go. I was beginning to think by hanging onto it, I was honoring my husband. In reality, it is just the opposite. By giving up the rage and forgiving whomever I thought had a part in it, I was honoring him.

The Lord began to show me by letting go of the anger, I could rise above it. I felt He was telling me to embrace the possibility of being open to healing, which I so desperately wanted. I was exhausted and it was time to reach out in forgiveness to those I thought had harmed me. I also needed to forgive myself. I could not do this right away but eventually, I did, and what a load it took off my back.

What would it take for you to stop struggling? How would it

feel to forgive others and forgive yourself, if necessary? Our Heavenly Father is sitting beside you. He is willing and able to help you. Ask Him, dear friend.

*In times of affliction,
we commonly meet with the sweetest
experiences of the love of God.*

~

Paul Bunyan

HOLIDAY GRIEF

I am now a member of a club no one wants to belong to. It's only been a couple of months since my husband passed away. My children and I are grieving. Our hearts are sad. Christmas is coming and, unfortunately, I can't stop it. The family traditions we have always looked forward to are no longer. So, what do I do? It's obvious, I must find a new way of celebrating (not the correct word for what I am feeling). Tonight, I have decided to paste on a smile and spend a few minutes at my neighbor's holiday party. I realize I must push myself a bit.

It's okay, dear friend, to be sad during the holidays. The first Christmas after losing a loved one is anything but merry. There are other times such as Thanksgiving, Easter, birthdays and especially the anniversary date of your loved one's death that often catch you by surprise. I learned if I didn't plan ahead, the anticipation was worse than the actual event. In the first few years, I planned a trip at Christmas. That worked for a while. Then there came a time when my children and I wanted to re-build our holiday traditions. We realized there would always be an emptiness, but as we looked for new ways to honor the memory of our loved one, our hearts began to beat a little lighter. Our gracious Lord is with you as you face the holidays and special dates. Lean on His strength, and in time your heart will also begin to beat a little lighter.

So do not fear,
for I am with you;
do not be dismayed,
for I am your God.
I will strengthen you and help you;
I will uphold you with
my righteous right hand.

~

Isaiah 41:10

FEAR

I have lost my tether and I am frightened. The fear I feel upsets my stomach. My brain is wired and I constantly question myself. Can I live alone? How can I be both mother and father to my children? Am I able to take care of my finances?

A quote by C.S. Lewis reads, "No one ever told me grief felt so like fear." I have found this quote to be true. Grief IS fear and it has a way of latching on and not letting go. When my husband died, everything changed. My life was turned upside down. Everything was unknown. Everything was awful. I never imagined fear, apprehension and sadness could be so intense.

I believe fear is our greatest struggle when grieving. Feeling afraid is a common response. However, it feels anything but natural. We all grieve differently. You may or may not be paralyzed by fear as I once was. If you are, please be patient with yourself. This too shall pass.

If you feel lost and can't find a place for yourself, reach out to someone. I found that a wise counselor, caring friends, or family members were always willing to listen. We even laughed at times, which helped put things into perspective. I also wrote in my journal each day. Writing seemed to strip away the overwhelming thoughts to make room for clarity.

The magic wand I hoped would appear to make this dreadful time go away alluded me. It wasn't there, but God was. I found the only thing I could do was to be patient, keep putting one

foot in front of the other, and trust in my Heavenly Father to see me through.

Please know I am praying for you, dear friend. God is sitting beside you. Lean into Him and ask for His help.

With our writing,
we honor the extent of our losses.
We give details, we exaggerate, we express our
pain, we share our greatest fears.
Through writing, we discover unexpected
particles of truth that light our path;
we move through our grief mindfully,
in a way that allows us to comprehend
and integrate the experience into our lives.

~

"Writing to Heal the Soul" by Susan Zimmerman

JOURNALING

I am now journaling. I am doing this out of desperation because I need to somehow stop the hurt. I am willing to try anything. So, I am keeping a notebook and pen beside my bed and I wake up each morning and I write. I started with a sentence or two which morphed into a paragraph and now I am filling three full pages.

I am finding this daily ritual to be a way to confront the mountain of my emotions that are all huddled together...anger, denial, remorse, depression, fear and so many more. The more I write, the more I notice my racing thoughts are slowing down. I think I have found the safe space I have been searching for. A place to simply be with my hurting heart.

Please try journaling, dear friend. I now believe journaling was the catalyst for my healing. Connecting my heart with my hand forced me to be present with my feelings. Writing a little or a lot each day, I was soon able to look back and recognize I was making a bit of progress. I was remembering and letting go at the same time.

The poet William Wordsworth said, "Fill your paper with the breathings of your heart." You can buy a beautiful journal, or like me, you can write in an 8x10 spiral notebook, using your favorite pen. I believe it's important to write in longhand and to keep the pen moving across the page. This allows you to push out what is churning inside you. There is no need

to be concerned with spelling or grammar. Just keep filling the pages.

Your journal is private, just between God and you. It is an opportunity to be honest about your feelings and to express your pain. You may feel sad after writing, but that's ok. Tears are important to the healing process and God is always beside you. Your heart knows what it needs to heal. Through your journal, I believe you will find the way.

The Lord himself goes before you
and will be with you, he will never leave
or forsake you. Do not be afraid.
Do not be discouraged.

~

Deuteronomy 31:8

DEPRESSION

Today I want to pull the covers over my head and sleep until this dreadful thing is over. I am exhausted, I have no appetite and no interest in anyone or anything. I am depressed.

Depression can be a constant visitor during the grieving process. You may feel isolated, sad and uninterested in life. Loss of appetite, sleeplessness and disinterest in everything except thoughts of your loved one are often symptoms. You may also find it difficult to concentrate. The term "out of focus" best describes this feeling. If you have a history of depression, I urge you to seek professional help. However, for most of us, it is the price we pay for the ability to love others and miss them desperately.

Dark days never last. However, we often wallow in the big question, "When will grief end?" I wish I could answer your question, dear friend, but it's different for each of us. I do know it's important not to rush the process. In order to heal, you must allow yourself to lean into the sadness and pain.

Instead of wallowing in the pit, perhaps it is time to take baby steps. This will help you move forward in increments. The big picture is much too overwhelming.

This is your opportunity to lie in green pastures and rest in God's presence. Our Lord has a great capacity for compassion. His light shines brightest in the darkness.

You may need to "dose" yourself,
taking short periods to really feel your pain
and then distracting yourself from it again,
so it doesn't overwhelm you.

~

Alan D. Wolfelt, Ph.D.

INTENTIONAL GRIEVING

My tear-stained journal is getting a lot of use these days. I am told by a friend who has experienced multiple losses, it is important to set aside time each day to intentionally grieve. I ask myself, "Who wants to do that?" Yet, in my heart, I know I must allow time to be with the pain. Writing down everything I've lost starts a flood of tears. I sob and cry as I remember the gifts my husband brought to my life.

I would encourage you to try intentional grieving, my friend. Many times, I would write in my journal. Other times, I would sort through photographs or letters. Allow yourself some time each day to do this. Then close your notebook and put things away.

An emotional wound requires the same attention as a physical wound. It's important that you lean into the pain and experience the emptiness and despair. Be willing to surrender to your grief, quiet the questions of why, and cry until you are finished. Tears are cleansing and are a much-needed release.

In the book of Ecclesiastes, we are told, "*there is a time to weep.*" This is such a time. Losing a loved one speaks to the very core of our being and we must allow ourselves to feel the sadness. This is not a time to be brave.

The Elephant in the Room
By Terry Kettering

There's an elephant in the room.
It is large and squatting, so it is hard to get around it.
Yet we squeeze by with, "How are you?" and,
"I'm fine," and a thousand other forms of trivial chatter.
We talk about the weather. We talk about work.
We talk about everything else – except the elephant in the room.

There's an elephant in the room.
We all know it is there. We are thinking about the elephant
as we talk together.
It is constantly on our minds. For, you see,
it is a very large elephant.
It has hurt us all.

But we don't talk about the elephant in the room.
Oh, please, say his (her) name.
Oh, please, say his (her) name again.
Oh, please, let's talk about the elephant in the room.

For if we talk about his (her) death, perhaps we
can talk about his (her) life.
Can I say, his (her) name to you and not have you look away?
For if I cannot, then you are leaving me...
alone...
in a room...
with an elephant.

ELEPHANT IN THE ROOM

I've noticed something recently. No one mentions my husband's name. This makes me sad because I want him to be remembered. I want to talk about him with friends and family, to laugh at the funny things he said and did. I just want to hear his name. It reminds me of that old poem, "An Elephant in the Room."

Elephants are known to take great interest in their deceased. They mourn just as we do. They are also known for having great memories. I believe if we could understand them, they would share precious moments about their loved ones.

Death, dying and grief are a part of life. Death is a mystery, something we will all experience at one point in our lives. One of the many benefits of speaking openly about our deceased loved ones is we begin to unravel the mystery of death. Talking about death is a conversation about life.

Henry Wadsworth Longfellow said, "There is no grief like the grief that does not speak." I would urge you, dear friend, to be courageous and speak of your loved one when you are in the company of others. They may be embarrassed at first, but so be it. This is not a time to think of their feelings, but to own your own. The hunger for memory is very prevalent when we are grieving. Do not deny it. Let's make friends with the elephant.

When I trust deeply that today God is truly
with me and holds me in a divine embrace,
guiding every one of my steps, I can let go
of my anxious need to know how tomorrow
will look or what will happen next month
or next year. I can be fully where I am
and pay attention to the many signs of
God's love within me and around me.

~

Henri Nouwen

ANXIETY

Today I am feeling overwhelmed. My heart is racing, and my thoughts are running wild. Anxious seems to be my middle name. I try to calm myself, to no avail.

Do you have days when you feel apprehensive and fearful? I learned that each day brought a new landscape. Some days I was up and about and feeling confident. Other days, I felt unsettled and found myself fretting over something as simple as going to the grocery store. I was on a roller coaster of emotions and I did not know which emotion would show up next.

God and patience are the only answers. Grief is not an athletic event with stopwatches timing your progress. It is more like slow dancing one step at a time. You may seem to be stuck in your grief, or even moving backward at times, thus the way of healing.

You may not realize it, but bit by bit you are making progress. Your job is to slow down, rest and continue to wait. Demanding this dreadful thing to be over only delays the process. Anxiety will end, my friend. The less you fight your restless heart, the easier it will become.

The Lord is on your side. He knows exactly what you are feeling, and He longs to help you. Try to be still and feel His presence. He wants to comfort you with His love and strength.

Each person's grief is as unique as their fingerprint. But what everyone has in common is no matter how they grieve, they share a need for their grief to be witnessed. That doesn't mean someone to try to lessen it or reframe it. The need is for someone to be fully present to the magnitude of their loss without trying to point out the silver lining.

~

David Kessler

GRIEF SUPPORT GROUPS

I am a grief group drop-out. I wanted to attend, but perhaps it was too soon. I was very uncomfortable and cried throughout the whole session. I felt embarrassed, fearful, ashamed of my feelings and I was reluctant to share. I've never been one to share my inner-most feelings.

Yes, it's true. I was a grief group drop-out. How sad for me. Had I been confident enough to continue, I might have found common ground with others who were also suffering. Looking back, I realize I wasn't ready to take advantage of the support offered to me.

I've learned through my training as a bereavement facilitator, it is better to wait at least a month before attending a group. It is hard to concentrate or even listen when we are so raw. I feel it is also important to attend a group where the facilitator is someone who has suffered a loss. She or he can empathize, and on some level, relate to what you are going through.

Grief is very lonely and isolating. You may feel no one cares or understands what you are going through. Attending a support group, you realize that others have similar feelings. Making connections with kindred spirits is very comforting. When we are brave enough to tell our stories and share our experiences, fears and struggles, we become mirrors for one another. We need and want to talk about our grief.

We all want to feel supported and cared about. I think

you will find this with a group of people who can relate to what you are experiencing. Grief is your own personal journey, but you don't have to go through it alone.

Support groups are not all doom and gloom. Sometimes we need to lighten up and we often do when we tell our stories. After all, there were times when we laughed and felt happiness with our loved one. Laughter is a great panacea. It is uplifting to express joy along with our tears.

There are other forms of support, as well. Books on grief, if you can concentrate, might be helpful. Journaling is very helpful. Caring friends who are willing to listen without giving advice, wise counselors, and especially those who have suffered a loss. However, I believe the most helpful is a support group. Sharing helps to lighten the load.

God is our greatest support of love and help. He is always willing to listen and help you find the peace you are so desperately seeking. Trust Him, dear friend.

A life with love will have some thorns,
but life without love will have no roses.

~

Anonymous

IDEALIZING

This morning I am pining for my sweet husband. I miss him and I miss my life before this devastating thing happened. The house is quiet. There is no laughter, no raised voices, nothing. I miss everything, even the times when he annoyed me. He was a good man with many admirable qualities, but he was not perfect. Neither am I.

It's only natural to idealize a loved one when they die. We sometimes put them on a pedestal and assign them a new character, one of perfection. While it is pleasant to remember our loved one as perfect, it is not realistic. They were human, and humans have commendable qualities as well as negative ones.

I would urge you to grieve the whole person, dear friend. The person you loved and the one who disappointed you at times. Someone who could be both awesome AND annoying. Healthy grieving is remembering all facets of our loved one.

You are not disloyal to remember the difficult times. You are human. Your loved one played many melodies on the heartstrings of your heart. Some high notes and some low notes. It's important to remember and celebrate them all!

"Because he loves me," says the Lord,
"I will rescue him, for he acknowledges
my name. He will call on me and
I will answer him; I will be with him
in trouble. I will deliver and honor him."

~

Psalm 91:14,15

PRAYER

*"The Lord is my shepherd, I shall not want."
Never in my life have I needed a shepherd more. I
am as helpless as a lost lamb.*

Prayer was no stranger to me. I grew up in the church,
memorizing the Lord's prayer and the 23rd Psalm. I was
taught to pray at a very young age. However, prayer escaped
me as I grieved for my loved one. I wanted to pray, but I
could not mouth the words. All I could say was, "Lord,
please help me."

Praying that simple prayer began the healing process. The
Lord heard my cry for help, and He came to my rescue. Of
that I am certain. I also found it helpful to read the Psalms
and pray over them. King David wrote many of these
beautiful verses. He was a man after God's own heart, but
he was also acquainted with deep grief and sorrow. He cried
out to the Lord in his distress. God was his comfort. Reading
what David wrote gave me hope that God would come to my
rescue and comfort me as well.

I urge you, my friend, to reach out to our loving Lord. Ask
Him to help you in your distress. He is ready, willing and
just waiting for you to call His name. He is a God of love,
comfort and peace. You do not have to travel the difficult
road of sorrow alone.

Hard times will always reveal true friends.

~

Unknown

HELPFUL HANNAH'S

I ran into a "Helpful Hannah" this week, someone I had not seen since my husband passed away. I sensed she was uncomfortable, but her words were stinging. "Please don't be sad. You are young, you will meet someone again soon," she said. My eyes filled with tears and not knowing what to say, I just nodded my head. The truth is, I have lost the love of my life and I am not looking for a new husband. I am devastated. How can I not feel sad?

You may have heard similar remarks such as, "It's time to move on." "He's in a better place." "Time is a healer." I've heard them all. Why do some people give unsolicited advice? It's because they are uncomfortable, and don't know what to say. Just saying "I'm sorry" doesn't occur to them. We have to give them grace. Most have never walked the path we are walking.

Then there are the friends who were a source of love and support. Friends who listened quietly as I poured out my heart. They never advised unless asked, and they never judged me. We all need angels by our side when life is tough.

As for the "Helpful Hannah's," I learned not to take them seriously. I also learned, if ever I was in their position, all I need to say is: "I'm sorry for your loss."

A lonely road goes nowhere
Days of nothing slowly fade
Softly staring through tears like raindrops
Hugging my knees in a chair by the window
Grieving

~

CD

HOMESICKNESS

This morning it is raining. Wrapped in a blanket, I sit huddled in my chair and watch the raindrops splatter on the window. I love the rain, always have, but today it reminds me of tears. I am homesick for my life as it used to be.

Nothing gets our attention like sadness. It follows us around like a puppy dog until we give it some attention. The homesickness I felt, and you may be feeling, is real. Let the sadness roll over you, my friend. It will have its say and move on. Be prepared though, for its return. How could it not? We all yearn for what was comfortable and precious in our lives.

Grief is like an echo. We are homesick for the past, but life calls us forward. We must remember the past, embrace the forward steps and reach for hope.

One thing I know, dear friend, is God eventually brings us into the sunlight. He did that for me. The tears I shed were washed in His promises of healing, purpose and joy. He wants to do the same for you.

By perseverance the snail reached the ark.

~

Charles Spurgeon

LONELINESS AND A NEW IDENTITY

This morning it occurred to me I have a new identity. I am no longer part of a couple. My children no longer have a father. I no longer have a husband. Who am I? I am suddenly single, lonely and frustrated.

As the days went by, loneliness washed over me in many forms. I pined for my husband in the quiet moments when I was reading the newspaper and wanted to share something I read. I missed having someone with whom to communicate my thoughts and ideas. Most of all, I missed his hugs.

I became frustrated when I had to make decisions on my own. Buying tires for my car or purchasing a new water heater drove me crazy. Simple things like waiting to buy a movie ticket would cause loneliness to steal over me. In my mind, I was the only one in line who wasn't part of a couple. The first time I ate in a restaurant alone, I felt as though everyone was staring at me. Thus, I would have a little "pity party." Can you relate, dear friend?

I found I could stay busy during the week, but the weekends were a different story. Having been in a couple's world for almost thirty years, I had few single friends. I pushed myself to join groups and take classes to hopefully cultivate new friendships. Meeting people with whom I had things in common increased my social circle, and the weekends became a little less lonely.

It didn't happen overnight, but eventually, with God's help, I began to embrace my new identity. I learned I WAS capable

of making decisions. There were times when I didn't make the best choice, but that was okay. I was growing stronger, and a new more confident me was emerging. Taking baby steps, I was moving toward healing.

*He has caused his wondrous works
to be remembered; the Lord is
gracious and merciful.*

~

Psalm 111:4

MEMORY BANK

I was only nineteen when he smiled at me from across the room. I will always remember his smile, so warm and wonderful. What else do I recall? I remember how he could skip a stone across a quiet pond without it sinking. He had a bumper sticker on his car that read, "It's never too late to have a happy childhood." He proved this when he tickled and wrestled with our children.

Beautiful experiences sustain us. They are forever, like looking through a photo album or a scrapbook of remembering. In my mind's eye, I see them, the lovely and the painful. All are important. I never want to lose the pages of our life together.

The days and weeks pass. We do the hard work of grief and begin to move forward with life, eventually healing. Healing, however, doesn't mean forgetting. Our memories give us the traction we need to move in a positive direction. In our mind's eye, we play them over and over like a moving picture album. How fortunate we are to have them so close.

Memories of your loved one will support you, dear friend. Treat them tenderly, recall them often, and smile through your tears.

The unthankful heart discovers no mercies,
but the thankful heart will find in every hour,
some heavenly blessings.

~

Henry Ward Beecher

DROPLETS OF GRACE

In addition to writing in my journal, I am keeping a gratitude list. This is something I call, "Droplets of Grace." This isn't a phrase penned by me, but by a woman who lost her husband. She was sharing with me what helped her when she was grieving.

So, I'm writing in my journal each morning, and before I go to sleep at night, I am counting my blessings. As I record droplets of grace, I find I am grateful for small things that are beginning to make a big difference in my attitude. I am grateful to find my newspaper on the doorstep, along with a rose and a note of encouragement from a thoughtful neighbor. I am grateful for sweet laughter as I walk with a friend. I'm grateful for sleeping through the night. I am grateful for my faithful puppy, Gypsy, who never leaves my side.

Sometimes when we find ourselves at a frightening low, we need to stop and take notice of what IS working. Sure, we are sad, and we have every right to be. However, we can observe beautiful moments that come our way.

My friend, I urge you to start recording your blessings. I found just writing down a few each day, my attention was shifting from worry and sadness to the good in my life.

I believe gratitude is a gateway to God from Whom all blessings flow. And He is the One who is the perfect Healer, the perfect Rescuer, the perfect Savior. Trust Him, dear friend. He is nearer than you think.

*Three meals plus bedtime
make four sure blessings.*

~

Mason Cooley

SELF-CARE

Coping with this thing called grief is a full-time job. It haunts me day and night. My mind is on overload and I find it hard to remain calm even for a few moments. Sleep alludes me at night and my energy is zapped during the waking hours.

Yes, dear friend, grief is all consuming. It can be physically and emotionally draining and may compromise your immune system if you aren't careful. We grieve, but we must not neglect our health.

Common physical symptoms of grief may include migraine headaches, digestive problems, hives and even nausea. These symptoms are usually short lived. However, if they persist, it's time to make an appointment to see your family physician.

Proper nutrition is key. Nourishing, healthy meals provide the energy we need during the day. I found I could not eat very much at one time, but several small meals or snacks throughout the day worked as well. No more cold cereal for every meal. I needed something more substantial.

It's important to keep a "lights out" schedule and establish a relaxing bedtime routine. As tempting as it might be to use your computer or phone before bed, it can interfere with sleep by suppressing the production of melatonin. Limiting TV time might be helpful, as well. I found reading something uplifting helped to calm me and promote sleep.

During the day, I forced myself to take short walks in the

fresh air and bright sunlight. Feeling the warm sunshine on my back released much needed endorphins which gave me more energy.

Writing in my journal each day and spending time in God's presence stilled my mind and gave me peace. The Lord was my constant help and He can be yours as well. He longs to sit beside you as you cry, walk with you as you exercise and watch over you as you sleep. Lean into Him, my friend, and rest in His presence.

Beginning is a gift that
comes unbidden
but ending can be crafted
like an art.
What lies beyond is mystery,
and hidden,
ending can be a wholeness
of the heart.

~

Pat Schroeder

DANCING WITH GRIEF

These days I feel like I'm dancing. One day I'm waltzing forward, and the next day I am sliding back. I find myself in the land of longing. I want to dance my way forward, but the two steps forward, one step back, keep moving from joy to woe, from light to dark.

Can you relate, my friend? Do you feel this way as well? If so, please be gentle with yourself and try not to become discouraged. Soon you will notice these erratic movements take more steps forward than back. Then you will realize healing has begun. There is power in the backward steps. We need them to propel us forward.

I would like to suggest you open your heart to gratitude. Any movement when grieving is a blessing. It is so easy to stay stuck. I've been there. I've questioned and whined and said, "Why me? Why do I have to feel this way?" Only our loving Lord knows the answer. He is gracious. Trust Him, dear friend, and give Him thanks for bringing you thus far.

No matter how long the winter,
Spring is sure to follow.

~

English Proverb

CHANGES IN THE LANDSCAPE

On my walk this morning, I discovered some changes in the landscape. I noticed a few blades of green grass peeking through the hard, brown earth of winter. I am wondering if this is a symbol for my hurting heart beginning to heal.

Seasons change, dear friend, and with them come growth and renewal. You may not think you are growing and getting stronger, but I believe you are. There will still be many days when you slip back into the familiar feelings of sadness.

However, they will become less and less as you begin to recognize you have a future, not just a sad past. You have relentlessly carried the heavy burden of grief for many months. Perhaps you need to pause, set your burden down for a moment, and remember the reason for your load. What does your pain represent? For me, it represented the devastation of losing someone I loved and cherished very much. I began to ask myself questions. Could I now carry this mass of grief with gratitude? Would I be willing to lay it down and feel nourished by beautiful memories? Slowly, the answers came to me. It was time to lighten my load and move forward while being grateful for the delicious joy of having loved.

The hard ground of winter was beginning to thaw. It can thaw for you as well. Embrace it, my friend. A wise person once said, "No winter lasts forever; no spring skips its turn."

Our psyches seem to protect us
until we are able to confront the pain,
and then the internal alarm clock rings,
telling us its time to wake up
and go to work.

~

Hope Edelman

EXERCISE

This black hole of tears where I find myself is physically and emotionally draining. However, today I am determined to do something about it. I'm questioning, "How do I get through this," instead of asking, "why me?" I must take over the reins of my life. If I want to become stronger, it's up to me. So, this morning I am dragging myself out of bed and lacing up my tennis shoes. I've decided to try exercise. My choice is walking.

I don't know about you, dear friend, but I desperately wanted to feel better. It was hard to get going some mornings, but I found the sunshine and fresh air lifted my spirits. Sometimes I listened to soothing music. Other days, it was just God and me, walking and talking.

Regular exercise, whether walking or exercising in a gym, is a potent mood lifter. Studies have shown people who exercise regularly are less likely to be depressed. A word of caution – there is no need to overdo it. Your body and emotions are still very tired. A thirty-minute walk or light exercise in a gym will be helpful, yet not sap your energy.

So, my friend, I want to suggest you lace up your tennies and hit the pavement. You will feel better for having done so.

He has made everything beautiful
in its time.

~

Ecclesiastes 3:11

CREATIVITY

I've discovered something. While being very diligent with my journaling, I'm also writing poetry. How did that happen? Reading poetry has never interested me, and now I'm writing it! The pages of my journal have turned into a creative outlet. I've found a place where I feel free to let go of the sadness for short periods of time.

A friend, who is a psychiatrist, once told me grief and the creative process go hand in hand. I now believe this to be true. I've also read studies of women who lost their mothers at a young age and later became recognized as authors, artists and even actresses.

Becoming famous is not the goal, but we can acknowledge and take advantage of the creative process. When we use our artistic imagination, we are free to go beyond our grief and pain.

Whether or not you feel you are creative is a moot point. It's not about impressing others. It's about living in the moment and escaping from the overwhelming sadness of your loss.

I like to write. Perhaps your choice is painting, singing, dancing or even making a collage. Gardening is a great outlet. Feeling your hands in the warm, rich earth as you plant flowers is very soothing. Whatever you choose to do, I believe you will find it beneficial. You deserve a break from your grief, a time to just be in the moment.

So, dear friend, be willing to pick up the pen, mix the paint

or just dance around the living room while singing at the top of your lungs. You will be glad you did. I can see God smiling!

"For I know the plans I have for you,"
declares the Lord. "Plans to prosper you
and not to harm you, plans to give you
a hope and a future."

~

Jeremiah 29:11

ENERGY SWEET ENERGY

Something occurred to me this morning. I am no longer fatigued. I am beginning to feel alive and filled with energy; positive energy that doesn't drain me as it did months earlier. The loss of my loved one has been devastating, but now I must look at it as an invitation to live.

How about you, dear friend? Are you beginning to regain your energy? Do you yearn for brighter days? I hope so. Staying stuck in grief is not what your loved one would want for you.

I'm certain you still have scars, and like me, they are visible on occasion. However, you can let them show and still move forward. The absentee landlord of your life has been silent far too long.

Do you dream of things you have always wanted to do? Would you be willing to nudge the door of your mind open a bit and create a wish list? Just the act of writing down your goals sets them into motion. Your dreams can be small or as large as you dare. They can be expensive or inexpensive. You can tiptoe, or go full speed ahead. The important thing is to open your clenched fists and begin to receive all the world has to offer.

God will be with you on your journey. Include Him in your plans and pray for His wisdom and guidance. He is ready, willing and able to help.

*There is a time to weep and a time to laugh,
a time to mourn and a time to dance.*

~

Ecclesiastes 3:4

GRIEF BREAKS

I am learning to take what I call "grief breaks." I realize there is still work to do, but right now I need a break.

I have always loved to dance. Dancing makes me happy. So, this morning I am turning up the music, twirling around the living room, and singing to the top of my lungs. I can't begin to tell you how this chased away the gloom and lifted me out of the echoing void in my heart. Doing something today that brings me joy is a much needed distraction. I'm certain the sadness will return, but in the meantime. . .I'm dancing!

You deserve a break as well, dear friend. Why not do something today that will bring you joy and distract you from the sadness that is so prevalent? You can count on grief to hang around. It doesn't go away until we finish the work. In the meantime, take a break. You deserve it.

Never be afraid to trust an unknown future to a known God.

~

Corrie ten Boom

A CRACK OF LIGHT

I am up early this morning. The soft light of summer peeks in through my kitchen window. It's peaceful, this crack of light, and I am grateful for another day. I am healing. I feel it as a puff of joy rises inside me.

It's been ten months since my sweet husband passed away. I've struggled with fear, sadness, anger and resentment. I now feel hopeful as a new, different me emerges. There is a wanting inside me to be filled.

Where are you in your grief walk, dear friend? Are you beginning to step into a new way of living? The open door God has placed before you is worth investigating. He opened the door for me, and it made all the difference. I learned to be bold, to ask for what I needed and to experience life in a way I never had. I had been sitting in silence for a long time and the new me was beginning to emerge. I was grateful for my change in attitude.

I learned everything we lose opens us up to more than we could ever imagine. There were many things I had always wanted to experience and now was my time. There were places I wanted to see, people I wanted to meet and groups I wanted to join.

I also realized it was time for me to lovingly share with others what I had learned on the grief path. It sometimes takes being in the darkest night to gain empathy and understanding for others. I'm rooting for you, my friend. Our Lord knows what it will take to remove the roadblocks so you can open yourself up to all He has in store for you. May it be so!

BRAVE WARRIOR

A legacy he left behind,
a brave warrior loving and kind.
He said,
"Don't cry for me,
whatever my fate
I've lived life abundantly.
I'm proud of you,
now please let me go.
I leave you with a gift,
the gift to grow."

~

CD

TIME

It's October and once again, the trees are losing their leaves. I watch out my window as they scamper and waltz in the wind. It's been twelve long months since my husband passed away. I now realize I am having more good days than not-so-good days. The emotional rollercoaster I have been riding is slowing down. I am grateful to feel less anxious and more at peace.

A question I am frequently asked is: "How long will grief last?" I wish I could tell you, dear friend. There are no clear-cut answers. We are all unique in our grief and the length of time it takes to heal is different for each of us.

For most, grief doesn't conclude at the one-year mark. However, it does soften. There were times the first year when I thought, "I've got this thing licked," only for it to come roaring back. I learned I didn't have it licked and probably wouldn't for a long time, if ever. It's very simple, we never forget but we can become strong and find joy again. In the meantime, I would urge you to trust in the One who longs to massage your heart.

No one escapes pain. We are constantly losing and regaining our balance. God has designed us to grieve. He has also designed us to cope and grow from the hard times we endure. Let's not waste the sorrow.

There are gifts hidden in our mourning. In the hard times of life, our character is invited to grow. We learn and become

stronger; people who are more loving, compassionate, and grateful for each day.

God had a plan for my life, and He has one for yours as well. We must untie the ribbons of our gifts and begin to move forward, celebrating the legacy of our loved one's life.

*I want you to hear my story and say,
"If she can do it, so can I."*

~

Dr. Edith Eger

LAST WORDS

$\mathcal{D}$ear Friend,

Today I am a happy and confident woman. There are times still when I wonder what life would have looked like had I not lost my loved one. However, I would not want to be someone other than who I am today.

Grief has been my greatest teacher. I now know I can survive the darkest night and still bask in the sunlight. I've learned to let gratitude flavor my days and embrace the joy of finding love again. Most of all, I've learned in every storm of life, I will find God's outstretched hand reaching for mine.

My prayer for you is one day, like me, you will wear the badge of grief with honor and triumph.

I wish you healing and abundant joy,
Carol Collins

I Wish to Thank...

the many participants who have attended my grief support groups over the years. You were a source of healing and inspiration to me as much as I was to you. I am grateful.

cdcollinspublishing@gmail.com

SELECTED READINGS

A Grief Observed by C.S. Lewis

Understanding Your Grief by Alan D. Wolfelt

A Grace Disguised by Gerald Sittser

Don't Take My Grief Away by Doug Manning

Grieving the Death of a Friend by Harold Ivan Smith

Motherless Daughters by Hope Edelman

Song of Sarah by Paula D'Arcy

Writing to Heal the Soul by Susan Zimmerman

The Choice by Dr. Edith Eger